A Desire For Disaster

by

Katie Proctor

First published 2022 by The Hedgehog Poetry Press

Published in the UK by
The Hedgehog Poetry Press
5, Coppack House
Churchill Avenue
Clevedon
BS21 6QW

www.hedgehogpress.co.uk

ISBN: 978-1-913499-57-0

A CIP Catalogue record for this book is available from the British Library.

Contents

Long Poem

Not all love affairs are supposed to last forever, but you're
immortalised in a long poem, and I don't write those. I don't
have the metaphors in me, but it's for the nonchalance, the
trains north to south joined like a paperclip chain made absent-
mindedly by wandering, ambitious hands, and the vending
machine pad that's still in my bedside drawer, coughing
and crying in the hotel bathroom. I write the long poem for
the knowing I'd look back and feel it in glimpses, the
bubblegum-aftershave taxi cocktail that got me drunk before
I knew how drunk felt, washing it out of my hair every night and
not knowing how to say goodbye, so not saying goodbye at all.
In the long poem I'm half the person I am now and double at
once, mystified and growing and learning a city in two weeks,
a chameleon in the dim light, double life, cool and off-white
and yellowed peach. The long poem lives in one room, four
walls and a Tesco sandwich that I couldn't taste, staying up
just to watch the ceiling: *I can't lose a moment of this, not
a single one, because it'll never be the same again.* It'll
be me out of here soon, out the rickety window and past
the pylons on the worn seat, and I know I won't ever let go
of this because it's the best and the worst thing in the world,
an explosive labelled *handle with care* but there's no touch
that's gentle enough to keep it right here, that feeling. In the
long poem it's not nearly as specific, as picture-taking,
obsessive memory-making; fourteen and too aware of how
I'm a curse and not a blessing, mutilated phrases that can
never get the little things quite right, the touch of thermals
against my bare skin, a cold Coke in the shopping centre and
a jigsaw making a picture of sweets, pink and green and *let's
keep her occupied, it'll be a long morning.* The long poem doesn't
end, just keeps going in folded towels and performances of hope,
crystals lined up and prayers in an empty bath. It keeps going in
love letters and anniversaries and rugs and train carriages,
and isn't it sad that I can't let go, eighteen, still clutching at the
crumpled up cardboard and wishing on falling stars in dreams
that are achingly lucid. I think it's just that, serial killing my own
story, no phone service in the woods and it's a good job nobody

ever heard of me anyway because I'll die here, right here in a
pile of falsified rubble. The long poem is the legacy of a fantasy
and a navy blue suitcase I can't empty. I look at my wrists and
their fluorescent veins that bloom like borderlines on a tissue
paper map, a long poem with a tenancy agreement stapled to
my skin. I love you, I think. It unravels, an emergency cord. I hear
it clatter on the tiles in someone else's room.

halogen / halcyon

I have looked at you through a screen, through techno
glitches that turn your face all the colours of neon.
And you are made like a halogen, halcyon, glowing
purple in a city backstreet. The front of a café and
the back of a club where people come to let the dark
web take over. Where people live computerised on
something implanted in the wrong side of their brain,
bleeding out electrics in the middle of a dance floor.
And I have seen you head to toe in metal casing
because you are more than human, and you are made
out of blood that glows luminous through the thin
sheet of your skin. Because you need something
stronger to hide the pain, a falsified excuse for a
cyborg. Like a single flicker behind an eyeball.
Pupils burning, soulless, meaningless without the
hardware.

Feathers and Wax (Ode to Icarus)

Maybe you're sitting at home in your jeans and sweatshirt
clutching a bottle like it's a lifeline, clutching at straws.
Maybe I have you all wrong and I'm reading it like I always
do, reading too much into the words that don't have meaning
unless you're the one saying them. Tell me everything's alright,
just like you used to, just a flicker of that cynicism I breathe in
like oxygen. Tell me you're coming back and you'll fix it, and
it'll be like you were never gone. I can hear it like a whisper, like
you were just here or maybe you still are, hiding somewhere
between the wooden floorboards, an echo, polar. Please
think of me, seeing my breath in an empty room where I used
to talk to you and the hours flew away like a white-winged
bird, feathers and wax. You were always there like a shadow,
a trace of social politics crouching in the corner behind my
poems, and now I don't think I can remember your face the
way I used to, when I would sit strumming an acoustic guitar
in a dimly lit bedroom. If the last was the way you looked on
my computer screen, pixelated, I'd say goodbye like you
were a bomb I couldn't defuse, about to decimate right there
in my kitchen. You used to steal away the early hours,
oblivious, and now I look up at stars that seethe silver asking
where you are, how many miles. Marco. Polo. I looked for a
word in that broken dictionary and I couldn't find a thing,
because I don't think there's a noun that would fix the way I
miss you, no citation in a library index. You've got my fingers
on strings, searching your name for things I can't tell you. The
truth, that I tried to fly to you but I got burnt, singed by the fear.
Unanswered questions that rattle like a pill I should have
taken but now I've lost my appetite. What if it's over? Did you
pick apart my skeleton, ivory on tile, and walk away with my
heart between your teeth? I've got pieces of you everywhere,
making holes in the carpet, I took without asking. An eye for
an eye, a soul for a glance.

the mess we leave behind

It started out like a shot in the dead of night, waking us from
the reverie we'd fallen into, five years' worth of complacency
wrapped up in two school uniforms, ties unfastened and
abandoned on the floor like we'd never heard of hesitation.
Because we never had, and it was the rush of it all that
planted the seed right there in that bedroom, your scent
orbiting me like a moth to a flame, clinging to my every
waking moment. And we were planets then, sun and
moon like the posts from 2012 described that I never
believed in, not until paper walls plastered in a rental flat
became the only thing I thought I could trust, and the
feeling of your bedsheets tangled up in our limbs became
my only real memory. Collective, codependent. But it
was the mess we left behind that made a cavity, my
sweet tooth like caramel, melting. It was the remembrance
of nights waiting for the water to wash you away, the
fear of gravity like cling film, glued to me in the heat of
the summer. I think of the healing, of the inches I grew
stepping out of you. The mess we left behind lingering,
an unmade bed, empty bookshelves. The ghost of you,
fading out of the pages.

portrait of devotion

if there comes a day where i do not love you, pick me orchids and remind me that devotion is a cosmic parasite and it's wrapped around my heart with silkworm threads. bathe me in rosewater with honeyed limbs, sweet and dark, and tell me that it's romantic to asphyxiate if it's you who abducts my air. spirit me away and call it illicit and star-crossed, and whisper, it'll be your mind that hurts the most, the bruised imitation echoing, you wanted this.

Snow Globe

On the other side of the world, where all the clocks are upside down, somewhere you are sitting, and maybe you are thinking about me. I imagine that I have crossed your mind once or twice; the time that you looked in the mirror and traced the red marks on your neck with concealer, and maybe when you took the kitchen scissors to your hair when you realised the dye from two summer ago finally grew out. I don't know if you miss me, and if I'm honest I don't know if I miss you either. But I wonder if you ever think about that night in July, pizza and blankets on the living room floor, when we didn't know it would be the last time we ever kissed each other goodbye. Tears could only turn to laughter and back again between those four walls when those planets were in orbit, and the stars were spinning backwards. Sometimes when the sky is turning midnight blue and I can see Cassiopeia, I think about the drive home that day, when I held your hand like I would never let go, and I cried all the way back to my bedroom. And I think about the moment I lost you, and how just then you meant so little. But you are always on my mind nowadays, as though you are the most persistent of winter storms, and I am living inside your snow globe.

Non-disclosure

You were temporary, a flicker of black on white like a bomb
in my hands, cold, too much to bear. A Thursday afternoon
in January, you chose me in shades of peach and blue,
slamming doors and feet slipping on stairs, and I didn't
have a chance to warn you that I wouldn't let go. Couldn't
let go, not with far off promises parcelled in khaki print and
obsessive-compulsive guesswork in the shape of "meant to
be," and I'm scared that you'll never leave, buried in my bones
and burning with the reminder of what could have been, what
my skin would look like under your floodlights in the dead of
night, somewhere in the fields I imagined dressed in borrowed
clothes. And I know you belong to someone else, someone
pretty that's crying in her bedroom like this was beyond her
wildest dreams. I felt you as you slipped away, a wasted
shot at satisfaction lingering in a camera lens, hours and days
waning like a prophetic moon. Yet still I dream, like it'll get
better and you're coming back. You're coming back. You're
coming back.

Betty (after Taylor Swift)

It's the fifties, and I'm standing in my prettiest dress
in the golden haze of a mid afternoon in May. Just
outside the door where your letters pile up every
morning is a single wilted rose, red like the lipstick
I wore on our first date. I remember when you
faked sick that day and ran to the garden where all
the flowers grew. You came to my porch covered
in plasters and I laughed like the world would end
tomorrow, and in that moment I swore I loved you.
Even though I told myself that sweet nothings at
seventeen are destined to melt like snowflakes on
two lovers' eyelashes in the first days of spring.
Right then I meant it. I meant it when you never
showed that evening, and I danced the night away
just thinking about you. And I meant it every
summer's day spent on my own, reading back
those poems and listening to those mixtapes. Now
your face is hard to see, but I think if you came to
my porch just like you did all that time ago I
would kiss you and believe every word you spoon
fed to my lips. But sometimes I wonder about
you and her, and I find I can't utter your name
without choking out a curse. The mistake I made
was letting you break my wings when you never
stayed to patch them up again.

Scratch Card

Learning to live with the right amount of hoping is like tearing a
scratch card in half, throwing potential and misery away with
the worst of the wasted. You cut yourself shaving and your face
looks wrong somehow, backwards in the prettiest of pictures
and empty, coming back to the sickness of mediocrity, and I swear,
I've tried it all. I've tried to believe in it, trust the cosmos and
stop waiting for the voicemails, searched for angel numbers and
a sign that things will turn out right, and it all ends on the bathroom
floor in that same ceaseless disaster, dulled by the tarot cards
and the opportunity. I've hung on to inevitable and beautiful,
crossed off days and made excuses for names I barely remember.
Cursed my best friends and made myself invisible, begging for
something, tell me I'm doing okay, tell me how to make it better,
where's the pill that fixes optimism? It lives in sweet nostalgia, a
taxi ride and an unfamiliar airport, learning the details of a memory
inside out, and it's twisted how quickly it disappears and I'm
losing the early minted mornings to vacancy. Yet I'm here like
a bruise, scarring and bloody, addicted to the alkaline purples of
the midnight sky, passed my sell-by date and sitting on the shelf,
peeling and crimson

Class of 2021

My body is filled with halogens standing
across from you, in lips fake kissed with
gloss. Maybe you could imagine they're
swollen, like I'm living my own life and
there's a lot you don't know, and it'd be
true if you hadn't penned a fable right
in front of me and broken the training
wheels with your borrowed black biro.
I could float away, snip the strings and
love and lose, drown you in tequila from
a champagne flute, an imitation of a
dizzy August under ultraviolet light. But
you would exist in the phrases I overuse,
and the poems I shouldn't write but
I do - I'm proud of them and I know you
would be too, but they're so close to home
that they'd be better off ashes. I'd kill
them in ceremony, sacrificial and settling
in the ridges in the tiles, on my hands, feet,
I'd say gone and forgotten, and it'd be
the flimsiest eulogy. I wish you'd stay,
wish you'd stick around and read them,
and it wouldn't be the way it is. Yet I am
helium in the liminal, minimal and pointless
with so much to say and so little chance
to be honest. For the sake of sedation.
You reside in the graveyard of my youth
and sexuality, making a home, and I buried
you but you claw your way out, half-alive,
a mindless reminder and perennial
permanence. It is customary, a hole in the
ozone. It doesn't stop.

.

Could Have

I remember you in a crowded room under rainbow
neon lights, looking at me like the world would end
tomorrow. I think about you often, in a borrowed
bedroom miles away from here, writing poems about
another girl that someone will read and scribble on
in red pen. *Call me by my first name.* I can feel the
yellow dress on my legs, grey cardigan and glitter
pooling on my cheeks in the heat, and the roses that
you planted in my stomach, thorns and petals, red
like the lipstick I put on in the car. Warm like the
touch of our skin in the backseat, your head on my
shoulder and the burning of twin hearts, white-hot
calescence. And I remember you sitting on a window
ledge, black patent leather touching crackling plaster
while I pour my agony into yours, two girls playing
with fire, running away before the niceties catch flame.
But I think about you as the one I could have had and
everything that could have been, kisses in the park and
swaying in a concert hall like a walking cliché. If
something had been different, all that time ago. The
moment gone in a flicker, flare, flashing, like a storm
and a forest fire. Burning out, an ocean of silver,
memories like cobwebs between us now.

Obsessive Compulsive

Hate how nobody has a clue
Why am I always explaining myself

Do I have to tell you
my brain isn't like yours
as if I don't say it enough

A problem shared is
a problem multiplied
until I have no problem
only all sentience bleeding
from a hole in my heart

realising
I gave up

"Just tell someone"
as if my soul doesn't beg for that
and as if it doesn't feel
like I'm flying for a second
before it all shatters

As if stains on pillowcases
don't talk to me at night

As if my neurones don't shriek
because your words sound like
my wildest dream

Imagine the thing you want most
is the thing you can't have
and if you break
your body breaks too

As if it isn't hard enough
on my own

and as if it isn't harder
when you tell me
"it will all be alright
you know you should just
talk"

life is a studio ghibli film

even the worst bits, or they try to be. the bits where my chest aches and the undiagnosed snake coils in my stomach, and i search for a reason to take a breath and notice the sky fading blue purple to black. the same colour as my bruises yet there's a rooftop scene right there, it's probably raining and the puddles are like mirrors shattering. and i hate the sky at night, hate the birds at dawn, it's got none of those van gogh galaxies and it's not so romantic when it's pointing out how wide your eyes still are. but i try when the tears come and the clock is glaring gaping orange. pretend like they are glittering on my cheeks, must be that stardust inside me. i'm not a lost cause just yet. it'd be more honest, maybe, sitting on a pavement in the early morning if the streets were lined with lanterns. but my sheets don't feel like mine after all these hours. there is little true about it.

Ode to San Francisco

The curve of her hips tastes like desperation
in the darkness of a bedroom somewhere in
San Francisco. She is listless, spine twisting,
Christmas lights glistening outside the frosted
window, propped open with a lopsided smile.
Bodies like bridges, elegant in the August
lowlight. Arms made as though a birdcage, a
million aluminium safety guarantees defying
solemnity, breakable like the ferns that line the
riverside. A woman made of magnets that bind
her to another's touch, alone, incapable of
letting go. When fireworks light up the sky she
does not look away. San Franciscan surprises
burning in her lungs after all this time.

Afterparty

When the girls come home from the party
spitting vodka and vomit, it is a cold
evening in October and the clouds are
heavy with the tears of the hopeless
and the drunk. The girl that holds her best
friend's hair back as she leans over
stained porcelain, tragic, is shivering on
the pavement in her jacket that smells
like someone else's boyfriend. The girls
that dance together after they were left
alone on the doorstep, are falling over
with their heels stuck in a roadside grate,
holding each other up, free and lost alike.
When the girls come home from the party
they are more than friends, holding hands
and leaving Kopparberg kisses on each
other's cheeks. Girls that are lovers in
pretty red dresses, that curl each other's
hair and paint their faces with the blush
of a thousand Sapphic violets.

Chloe

It was November and I was sitting in a skyscraper somewhere
in the south when I met you, a mid afternoon haze
crossing the skyline of the city, hands trembling with nerves.
Running on chocolate in a train carriage, the fear of losing
something I barely knew and an excuse for small talk in a
room with strangers. It was gone in minutes and then I
was doubled over in a bathroom, apprehension lighting
like a speck of a flame with the forethought I could
hardly acknowledge. You tasted like vanilla ice cream
then, saccharine, adrenaline mixed with the acidic paralysis
of loving you like a valentine without any semblance of
certainty. That winter day would have faded into obscurity
without me sitting in that corridor in the cold, my spotty
phone signal holding you just out of my reach, a mirage
vignetted at the edges. I was your polar opposite, like iron
filings magnetised in peaks, stalactites, blown over by
a whisper. Miles apart, because it was always meant to be,
no matter the nightmares that hung like fog over my dreams
for weeks. It could never be so right. You, faceless before I
met you, words on a page in black Courier searching for a
meaning. Living out of a suitcase for you, clothes on a hotel
room floor and a façade of a hospital bed, white sheets and the
smell of us. The smell of you. Tied to me, like a single thread
of gold between our hearts. Twins, a permanent memory of
reciprocal.

Acknowledgements

Long Poem was originally published by Yuzu Press.
Class of 2021 was originally published by Ice Lolly Review.
Obsessive Compulsive was originally published by HEBE magazine.
Afterparty was originally published by heartbroken zine.
Feathers and Wax (Ode to Icarus) and *Chloe* were originally published by Sledgehammer Lit.

About Katie Proctor

Katie Proctor (they/them) is a 19 year old poet from Yorkshire, England. They write freeform poetry and prose typically regarding their experience with love, relationships and mental health. They are the author of Seasons (2020), HELICOPTER HONEY (2022) and A Desire for Disaster (2022). They are the editor-in-chief of celestite poetry, a journal of creative writing. They are currently on a gap year, and will be studying English and Related Literature at the University of York in 2022. You can find them on Twitter and Instagram @katiiewrites and online at katiiewrites.carrd.co.